FROM PESTS TO PETS

HOW SMALL MAMMALS BECAME OUR FRIENDS

FROM PESTS TO PETS

HOW SMALL MAMMALS BECAME OUR FRIENDS

John Zeaman

Before They Were Pets

FRANKLIN WATTS
A Division of Grolier Publishing
New York London Hong Kong Sydney
Danbury, Connecticut

Cover and interior design by Robin Hoffman
Illustration p. 24 by Karen Kuchar
Illustrations pp. 16, 20, 28, 35, 43, 49 by Stephen Savage

Photographs ©: Animals Animals: cover bottom left (Richard Kolar), 6, 26 (Renee' Cuniculus), 41 (Robert Maier), 33 (Terry G. Murphy), 40 (Patti Murray), 30 (Robin Redfern), 48 (Renee' Stockdale), 12; Bridgeman Art Library International: 47; Comstock: 53 (Art Gingert), 14; ENP Images: cover center, 9 bottom, 35 (Michael Durham), 15 (Pete Oxford), 19 right (Konrad Wothe); Folio, Inc.: 8 (David Falconee), 9 top, 44 (Patricia Lanza); Photo Researchers: cover top left (Alan Carey), cover bottom right (Tom McHugh), 22 (Bill Bachman), 21 (E.R Degginger), 46 (Gregory G. Dimijian, M.D.), 31 (Hank Morgan), 23 (T. Walker), 42 (Jerome Wexler), 17; Sygma: 37, 38 (Pierre Perrin); Tony Stone Images: 51 (Kevin Horan), 36 (Chris Warbey), 52 (David Young-Wolff); Visuals Unlimited: 2 (Walt Anderson), 19 left (Stephen J. Lang), 13 (Milton H. Tierney, Jr.).

Visit Franklin Watts on the Internet at:
http://publishing.grolier.com

Library of Congress Cataloging-in-Publication Data

Zeaman, John.
From pests to pets : how small mammals became our friends / John Zeaman.
p. cm. — (Before they were pets)
Includes bibliographical references and index.
Summary: Provides an overview of how various small mammals—including gerbils, hamsters, guinea pigs, mice, rabbits, rats, and ferrets have evolved into animals that are kept as pets.
ISBN 0-531-20350-6
1. Pets—Juvenile literature.   2. Mammals—Juvenile literature. 3. Domestic animals—Juvenile literature. [1. Mammals. 2. Pets. 3. Domestication.]   I. Title.   II. Series: Zeaman, John. Before they were pets.
SF416.2.Z425 1998
636.9'35—dc21   97-26723
                                                                      CIP
                                                                       AC

CONTENTS

Some people believe this small mammal is an unwanted pest. Others see it as a lovable pet.

INTRODUCTION

If your town has a pet store, perhaps you've stopped there to look at the different animals for sale or to buy food for a pet. Like most pet stores, it probably has a variety of small, furry animals: fat guinea pigs, quiet rabbits, white rats, friendly hamsters, cheerful gerbils, and small mice. Maybe the owner even has a ferret that he lets out of the cage, its small, alert head glancing this way and that.

These pets are all small **mammals.** They belong to the same class in the animal kingdom that we do. Like us, they are **warm-blooded,** have hair, and feed their young milk. Those qualities, plus a number of similarities in bone structure, define us as mammals.

7

Despite the difference in size, these small animals are our relatives. We all evolved from the same mammals about 100 million years ago. Those mammals were about the size of a gerbil or a hamster.

But despite the affection we feel for these animals, our society's attitude toward them is confusing. Let's leave the pet store, a place where we can buy toys and food for mice and other small mammals, and walk down to the hardware store. There, on the shelves, are traps and poisons designed to kill mice and rats.

Although these animals are regarded as pets, as creatures to be loved and cared for, they are, in other situations, seen as pests. These animals do not have the special position in our lives that dogs and cats have. No one is permitted to kill and eat dogs and cats, as is the case with rabbits.

People love cats and dogs for their emotions and loyalty. Small mammals do not have such a close relationship with society.

In some households small mammals are treasured members of the family. In other households they are unwelcome guests to be poisoned, captured, or trapped.

Dogs and cats are intelligent and capable of emotions that seem like our own. Small mammals, however, still retain many of the qualities of wild animals. They spend most of their time in cages. They are captive animals. Most can't be housebroken, and they may run away if let loose.

How did these animals come to be pets? Each animal has a different story. Some, like rats and mice, were attracted to human settlements by the availability of food. They found convenient shelter in basements and beneath floorboards. Others, like guinea pigs and rabbits, were originally kept to be eaten. Gerbils and hamsters are recent additions to the human community, taken straight from their burrows into laboratories and from there to pet stores. The ferret was bred thousands of years ago, from a wild animal called a polecat, to catch mice, rats, and rabbits.

1
GUINEA PIG,
OR
CAVY

The guinea pig is not a pig at all, but a **rodent,** just like mice, rats, and squirrels. Like all rodents, it has chisel-edged front teeth, called incisors, which are good for gnawing. These teeth grow throughout its life and are self-sharpening.

No one is sure why they are called guinea pigs today. They were probably first called pigs because of their small fat bodies and insistent squeals. The other part of their name is more of a mystery. Guinea pigs were first brought to Europe about 400 years ago by Spanish sailors from Dutch Guiana in South America. Perhaps people confused "guiana" with "guinea." Or, perhaps it originated because

Pigs?

What do guinea pigs have in common with pigs? Like pigs, the males are called boars and the females are called sows.

A young guinea pig

Guinea is the name of the west coast of Africa, where ships carrying the animals often stopped before sailing on to Europe.

The guinea pig is also called a **cavy**, a name which is also used to describe some relatives of the guinea pig. The scientific name for the pet cavy is *Cavia porcellus*, which is Latin for "piglike cavy."

INTO THE HOME

The guinea pig was probably the first of the small mammals to be **domesticated.** Its ancestor, the wild cavy, was tamed as early as 5,000 B.C. by the tribal people who preceded the Incas in the Andes Mountains of South America. **Archaeologists** have found small statues of guinea pigs dating to this period. No one knows why these people made the statues, but it suggests that they must have admired or placed a special value on guinea pigs.

Certainly that was true of the Incas, the Andean people who lived in South America when Spanish **conquistadors** conquered them in the 1500s. The Incas performed sacrifices, religious rituals in which an animal, or even a person, was killed as a gesture to the gods. The Incas used guinea pigs as sacrificial animals. They also mummified their remains and buried them in the tombs of their kings and nobles. Perhaps the guinea pigs were

The wild cavy is the guinea pig's ancestor.

Guinea pigs show affection for each other and prefer to live in groups. Animals that live in groups are easier to domesticate.

Guinea Pig Language

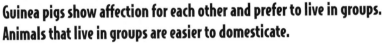

When guinea pigs want food or water, they often give a low or a loud whistle, or sometimes a grunt. They make a chuttering sound when they are angry or irritated. They squeal when they are frightened and murmur softly when they are happy.

meant to be food in the afterlife. Or, maybe the guinea pig was a very special or sacred animal to them, just like the cat was to the ancient Egyptians.

The guinea pig must have been very easy to tame. Wild cavies are extremely gentle animals. They live in burrows or hide in dense underbrush, and they have no defense from enemies other than to run for cover. They are also very sociable animals and live in large groups. Many of the animals that people have successfully domesticated, such as the dog or the horse, also live in social groups. Social animals are often able to transfer their bond with their own kind to people. Guinea pigs are not as intelligent as dogs or horses, nor do they have the complex social lives of those animals, but they do show affection for each other and they do communicate with a variety of sounds.

The wild cavy that the Incas tamed had short, coarse fur that was usually gray or reddish brown. This type of fur is called **agouti**. However, the drawings and descriptions of the Spanish conquistadors show that the Incas had already bred guinea pigs with fur of several different colors.

These tamed guinea pigs were kept as food animals, but they were probably also kept as pets. Today, the native people who live in this same area allow guinea pigs to scavenge freely around their huts. When they wish to eat one, they catch it and kill it.

These guinea pigs are kept for food on a South American farm.

15

COMING TO EUROPE

The Spanish brought guinea pigs back to Europe as a new food animal, similar in size and apparently in taste, to the rabbit. By the 1600s, they had become a popular table delicacy in Germany. It wasn't until the guinea pig reached Britain in 1750 that it became a pet.

Since that time, their gentle nature has made guinea pigs popular pets all around the world. They are also used frequently in medical research, so much so that the phrase "guinea pig" is used to describe someone on which something new is being tried out.

BREEDING

Today, there are about twenty different varieties of domestic guinea pigs. They come in brown, black, tan, and orange. There are also **albino** guinea pigs with all-white fur and pink eyes. Another type of white guinea pig has dark ears, feet, and nose. Tortoiseshell guinea pigs have fur that is a combination of two or three colors, such as black and brown and white, or orange and black.

Guinea pigs have also been bred with different kinds of fur. The most common type is the short-haired guinea pig. Its fur is short and coarse and lies sleekly back against its body. Others have a fluffy crest on top of their

heads. The Peruvian has long, silky hair that hangs down to the ground and makes the animal look like a mop. The Abyssinian has hair that grows in curls over its body, as if it is covered with cowlicks.

Peruvian guinea pigs have long, flowing hair.

CHAPTER 2
RABBITS AND HARES

At one time, scientists classified rabbits and hares as rodents because they have chisel-edged gnawing teeth. But rodents have only two pairs of these teeth, while rabbits and hares have three pairs. Because of this, and a few other differences, these animals are now grouped separately.

Both rabbits and hares have long ears and long hind legs, but wild hares are generally larger than rabbits, and their ears and legs are longer. Hares are also more solitary than rabbits and live above the ground. They don't burrow like rabbits.

Wild hares (below) tend to be larger than rabbits (left).

RABBIT GARDENS

No one knows who first domesticated rabbits, but the European rabbit has been kept and reared by humans in a semi-captive state for at least 3,000 years. The Romans kept them in warrens or "rabbit gardens." They also used similar enclosures to keep snails, bees, and large mammals such as deer. Rabbits were raised both as food and for their pelts, which were sewn together to make warm clothes.

Keeping rabbits must have seemed like a great discovery to people. No longer was it necessary to go out and hunt or trap rabbits, which are swift and evasive animals. All a person had to do was catch a mating pair, put them in a cage, and wait. Rabbits reproduce very quickly. It only takes a month for baby rabbits to develop within the mother, and each litter usually produces three to nine "kittens."

Keeping rabbits this way was not really the same as taming them. Within these rabbit gardens, the animals dug their own burrows, ate food that was grown or left for them, and lived almost the way they do in the wild. When a rabbit matured and fattened up, the people ate it.

WORLD TRAVELER, WORLD PROBLEMS

As wild animals, rabbits lived in Spain, southern France, and perhaps North Africa. But the Romans took them to every land they conquered, and soon rabbits were being kept all over their vast empire. Because of their burrowing abilities, many rabbits escaped into the countryside and took up residence in places where rabbits had never lived before.

This is why some places have had wild rabbit population explosions. When there are too many rabbits, they overrun gardens and farms, eat too much vegetation, and become a nuisance to people. This happened in Australia when the early colonists brought rabbits to the continent for the first time. Rabbits soon spread everywhere.

Rabbits were spread further when sailors left them on islands to **breed** and provide a store of fresh meat for any passing ship. Other people set up "rabbit colonies" on small islands where the animals could breed freely and also be easily rounded up and captured. As a result, rabbits are now found on islands all over the world.

Conies

Rabbits were called conies by Europeans. They earned that name because they made tunnels, which are called cunniculos in Latin. For this reason the enclosures rabbits were kept in were called coneygarths, or "rabbit gardens."

Rabbits reproduce very quickly, which has caused problems in places where rabbits have no enemies.

Raising rabbits in rabbit gardens was so easy that many people in the 1800s tried to make a business of it. But soon, so many rabbits were being raised by people that there were more rabbits for sale than people wanted. Plus, rabbits were escaping and multiplying so fast that they were easier for people to catch on their own. By 1880, rabbits were so plentiful in the English marketplaces that rabbit farmers were forced to lower their prices until they couldn't make money anymore. By 1900, rabbits were one of the most common animals in England and people were trying to figure out ways to get rid of them.

The rabbit population in some parts of the world is so large that people must capture rabbits every year.

There are so many rabbits in the world today, that it's easy to forget that they once lived only in one corner of southern Europe. The rabbit's population, like the horse's, has greatly increased as a result of being tamed by people.

Rabbits and hares have adapted to different habitats all over the world.

23

WHAT ARE A RABBIT'S EARS MADE OF?

Everyone can easily identify a rabbit by its ears. But what are its ears made of?

If you touch your own ears, you will feel a hard but flexible tissue. This is called **cartilage**. Cartilage is not bone. It is soft and bends without breaking. Like ours, a rabbit's ears are made of cartilage. In the diagram below, you can see that the rabbit's bones do not extend into its ears.

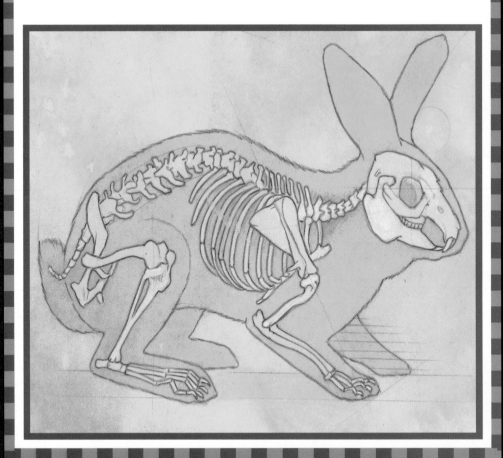

As happens with all animals that are kept captive, people grow attached to some and keep them as pets. During the Roman period and later, children had plenty of opportunities to play with rabbits and to convince a parent to let them keep a favorite. Perhaps there was a sick rabbit that needed care, or a runt that was excluded from the litter, or one that was born with unusual colors or fur that made it seem too special to kill.

One way or another, rabbits found their way into the human community as companions, as well as a source of food and skins. They are gentle animals and are easy to tame and keep. Like guinea pigs, they live in social groups and show affection and cooperation with each other, a quality that always helps animals form attachments to people.

BIG AND BIGGER

Rabbits were so easy to raise and fatten that, for a long time, people didn't try to make them bigger the way they did with pigs, cows, horses, or other animals. It wasn't until around the year 900 that people began to breed rabbits selectively.

This was first done by European monks who kept rabbits in their monastery courtyards as a source of food. The monks chose the largest rabbits and put them together to mate. As they continued to do this, the rabbits of each generation grew larger. The result was a bigger rabbit with a larger face.

Today, the rabbits found in Spain, which are descendants of the original wild rabbits, are smaller than those in the rest of Europe. Other rabbits are bigger because they are descended from rabbits that were bred to a larger size and then escaped into the wild.

Fighting Rabbits

Although rabbits are considered timid creatures and are easy for people to handle, they can be quite valiant in a fight. A rabbit doe, or female rabbit, will often fight fiercely to protect her young from a predator. Bucks, or male rabbits, will also fight with each other, sometimes causing serious injury or death.

The ears of Lop rabbits are too heavy to be held straight up.

By 1900, people were breeding rabbits in all kinds of sizes and shapes. They were no longer just trying to make rabbits bigger with more meat and larger pelts. As happened with dogs and cats, people began to enjoy the novelty of new breeds.

Today, there are about ninety recognized breeds. Some "giant" breeds can weigh as much as 20 pounds (9 kilograms)! At the other extreme is the 14-ounce (400 grams) "mini-rabbit," bred in France as a pet for children who live in small apartments. Rabbits have also been bred with different size ears. A breed called the Lop has gigantic ears that usually measure about 23 inches (59 centimeters). Because their ears are so large and heavy, however, the rabbits cannot raise them and move them the way other rabbits can.

CHAPTER 3

RATS

Black and brown rats are the only rodents that are not commonly eaten by people anywhere in the world. Perhaps this is because they are scavengers that eat garbage or because they have a reputation for carrying disease.

BLACK RATS

Indeed, the black rat is believed to have caused a greater number of deaths among people than any natural disaster or war. The most serious disease it spread is **bubonic plague** (Black Death), which wiped out millions of

people during the fourteenth and fifteenth centuries. The disease was actually spread by fleas, which jumped from rats to people and passed on the infectious bacteria. Black rats can also spread typhus, food poisoning, and rabies.

The black rat is an excellent climber, which enabled it to scramble aboard ships via the ropes that tied the ship to the dock. It originally came from Asia Minor, but it's ability to stow away on ships allowed this animal to spread all over the world.

In this illustration of the Black Death, people flee the disease in a carriage while a skeleton, representing death, prepares to strike them down.

BROWN RATS

The brown rat, also called the Norway rat, is larger and more of a burrower than the black rat. It is also a good swimmer. Its original home was probably along stream banks in eastern Asia. It spread across Europe in the mid-1500s and reached Great Britain around 1720. Once brown rats began to live in European cities in large num-

Bigger and stronger, the brown rat pushed the black rat out of the cities.

bers, they drove out the smaller black rats, who then moved back to the ports and onto ships. The brown rat is probably one of the most successful animals in the world. It will live anywhere, even in sewers, and eat anything. It can gnaw its way through wood, stonework, and metal plates in order to get at food. It thrives in both cold and hot environments and can survive with very little food.

Despite many people's fear of rats, they are the intellectuals of the rodent world. They are very cunning, adaptable, extremely curious, and love to explore. For this reason, rats have often been used by psychologists in learning experiments. They are very good at learning mazes, and they can also solve problems such as learning to recognize a particular letter of the alphabet.

While a scientist takes notes, this rat searches for food.

SMART RATS

Wild rats have been observed doing many intelligent things. They have been seen helping each other roll stolen eggs back to their nest. In one case, a group of rats formed a line from an egg basket to their hole and proceeded to hand the eggs from one to another in their forepaws. Rats also show a devotion to the handicapped members of their own kind. Observers have seen old blind rats helped along by their companions during migration. In one case, a rat was seen leading a blind female with a length of rope that each held in its mouth.

Largest Rat

The largest brown rat ever recorded was killed in 1881 and measured 23 inches (55 cm) in length and weighed 44 ounces (1.2 kg).

FANCY RATS

Brown rats are the ones that are domesticated as pets. They are usually bred to be white, or albino, and are called "fancy" rats, which is another way of describing a pet animal that has been changed by breeding. These fancy rats are much friendlier than wild brown rats because they have been bred from gentle rats. This process is know as **selective breeding**. To create a more gentle breed of rat, people selected individual rats that were friendly. They then mated them with similar rats. Eventually, after many generations, a gentler breed of rat resulted.

The first person known to have bred rats was a man named Jack Black, the official rat catcher to Queen Victoria of England. This happened in about 1850. He noticed

Most rats sold in pet stores today are albino.

that albino and other oddly-patterned brown rats were sometimes caught in his traps, and he decided to breed some in captivity.

Today, most pet rats are albinos. They are the largest variety and are the ones usually sold in pet stores. Rat breeders have not been able to create the wide variety of colored fur that is found in specially bred mice. Other varieties are the Japanese hooded rat, which comes in several distinct colors and has black or ruby eyes, the Siamese rat, the Himalayan rat, the Red rat, and the Irish Black rat.

Short Life Spans

Rats in the wild live only about 1 or 2 years. In captivity, the life expectancy of an albino rat is about 3 years.

CHAPTER 4
THE MOUSE

Mouse Vision

Mice have round bulging eyes to see all around them, but they cannot see things very well at a distance. They are extremely nearsighted.

The house mouse is the second most numerous mammal on Earth after humans. It is also the most widely distributed of all mammals. Wild mice are found on every continent, including Antarctica. They are extremely adaptable and have been found living in the least promising places, even inside meat refrigerators!

Like other rodents, mice have chiseling front teeth for gnawing. They also have cheek pouches for carrying food, a keen sense of smell, large ears, and eyes that stick out of their heads for all-around vision.

Mice are hunted by an unusually large number of animals. Hawks, owls, snakes, foxes, coyotes, cats, raccoons, and other **carnivores** all depend on mice for food. The mouse relies on its sharp vision, hearing, and quick reflexes to escape from enemies. We say "timid as a mouse," but despite that expression, mice can be quite brave, often fighting animals larger than themselves when cornered.

OUR CONSTANT COMPANIONS

Mice live with people whether we want them or not. Because their lives are so intertwined with people today, scientists are not even sure where mice originated as wild animals.

The house mouse has linked its life to humans.

35

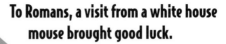

To Romans, a visit from a white house mouse brought good luck.

The house mouse was well-known to the Romans. Roman naturalist Pliny the Elder wrote that a visit from a white mouse would bring good luck.

Despite the fact that the male mouse has an unpleasant smell, mice have been tamed and kept as pets for at least the last 300 years, and some scientists believe that mice were kept as pets from early Roman times. Since mice live as wild animals in people's homes, finding mouse bones in a house does not tell archaeologists whether that animal was a pet or a pest.

Saved by the Bite?

The ancient Greeks used to encourage mice to bite them because they believed that a mouse bite cured illnesses.

FANCY MICE

Like rats, specially bred mice are called "fancy mice." The first fancy breeds of mice were developed by the Japanese in the 1600s. The National Mouse Club in England was founded in 1895, and today the club recognizes forty breeds of mice in a great variety of colors and patterned coats. The group sponsors shows, just like dog and cat shows, that give prizes for unusual varieties or perfect examples of a particular breed. The satin variety, for example, has a particularly shiny coat. The seal-point Siamese mouse has markings similar to the seal-point Siamese cat. Some breeders have created large mice that

measure up to 11 inches (25 cm), making them larger than the brown rat.

Today, the newly popular sport of mouse racing has encouraged people to breed mice for speed. In mouse racing, mice compete on elaborate 12-foot (3.6-m) obstacle courses, with water jumps and other obstacles. People bet on the outcome of the race, just as they do in horse racing. The white mice that run these courses are called

SINGING MICE

Mice are musical animals. They sing long songs, but normally their voices are too high-pitched to be heard by human ears. Only when a mouse is sick and its voice is affected can people hear its song. In 1946, a singing mouse with a voice that could be heard from a distance of 60 feet (20 m) was exhibited in London. Since then, hundreds of stories have been published about mice with singing ability. Their singing voice sounds like a weak canary, with a single song sometimes lasting as long as 10 minutes.

"thoroughbreds." Unfortunately, mice do not run as predictably as horses. Often they just sit down on the track and clean themselves. They also have been known to scurry along the track and back again without crossing the finish line.

The winner

CHAPTER 5 — HAMSTERS AND GERBILS

HAMSTERS

The golden or Syrian hamster is the world's most popular small pet. That's surprising, because these animals weren't domesticated until 1930. An Israeli zoologist, Dr. Israel Aharoni, was on an expedition in Syria in search of new animals to use in laboratory research. He captured several gray hamsters, but then local people told him about a different hamster, one with reddish fur.

He dug in the fields where these hamsters had been sighted and eventually found a mother with a litter of twelve babies. He took them back to his laboratory where he hoped to breed them as laboratory animals. Some of

39

The golden hamster is a recent addition to the pet world.

Hamster Habits

Hamsters are nocturnal animals. They sleep all day and wake up in the early evening.

the hamsters escaped from their cages, but after about four months the first golden hamsters were born in captivity.

As more were raised, they were sent to other laboratories in France, England, India, Egypt, and the United States. The hamsters began to live and multiply in laboratories all over the world. The scientists who raised them began to notice that these little animals quickly became tame and friendly. Some of the scientists took extra hamsters home as pets for their children. Pet dealers learned about these new animals and began to breed and sell them. By the 1950s, hamsters had become the hottest new pet craze.

It's remarkable that every pet golden hamster today is a descendant of that female that was dug up in Syria in 1930.

The name "hamster" comes from the German word hamstern, which means "to hoard." Hamsters have huge cheek pouches that they can fill with seeds or other food. They take the extra food back to their underground burrows and hoard it away in food-storage chambers.

Hamsters are rodents. They are closely related to rats and mice and are between them in size. There are four main types of hamsters: the common or European hamster, the golden or Syrian hamster, the gray hamster, and the dwarf hamster. The golden hamster has been the most successfully domesticated.

Most hamsters are solitary, aggressive rodents, but the golden hamster is fairly gentle and easy to handle. Its solitary lifestyle also makes it adapt well to living alone in a tank or cage. In fact, two adult hamsters will fight if kept together in the same cage.

The hamster gets its name from its enormous cheeks, which it stuffs with food.

41

Hamsters can be
very playful.

Hibernating Hamsters

During the winter a hamster hibernates. Its body functions slow down and it appears to be in deep sleep. From time to time it wakes up and nibbles some food it has stored nearby.

HAMSTER BREEDING

Hamsters are very fast breeders. It only takes sixteen days for a baby hamster to grow within its mother before it is born. Anyone who tries to keep a mating pair of hamsters as pets will soon have a rodent population explosion. It has been estimated that, under perfect breeding conditions, a pair of hamsters could end up with 100,000 descendants in a single year.

As with the other small mammals, hamsters have been bred in different colors and fur types. There are albino hamsters, and albinos with black ears. The piebald hamster has white spots on its body and a white streak down the center of its face. Long-haired hamsters are called teddy-bear hamsters. Other hamsters are cream colored or bright cinnamon-orange. Another type has a white band around its middle.

GERBILS

Gerbils are closely related to hamsters and are very similar in appearance. They also live in underground burrows in sandy, sparsely vegetated areas, eat similar foods, and reproduce at a rapid rate. Some **species** of gerbils are native to the Middle East, where the golden hamster comes from. But the only type of gerbil that has been tamed in North America is the Mongolian gerbil or clawed jird. Its native habitat is the Gobi Desert of northeastern China and Mongolia.

Gerbils are even more recent additions to the pet community than hamsters. In 1935, a Japanese zoologist collected twenty pairs from the Amur River basin on the Chinese-Russian border. From Japan, eleven pairs were sent in 1954 to the United States to be used in medical research. In 1964, it was launched as a pet on the American market, and like the hamster, it has become enormously popular with the public.

Gerbils have an even gentler disposition than hamsters, which can sometimes nip their owners. For this reason, pet store owners often refer to them as "gentle gerbils." Gerbils are also more sociable than hamsters and are not so content to live as solitary pets. Keeping a breeding pair, however, will cause the same kind of population explosion as hap-

Why "Gerbils?"

The word gerbil means "jerboa-like." The jerboa resembles the gerbil but is a larger rodent that leaps like a miniature kangaroo.

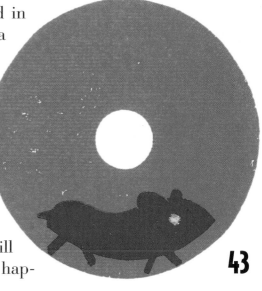

Gerbil Burrows

In the wild, a gerbil colony will live in a burrow complex that is usually about 10 x 14 feet (3 x 4.2 m) with six or seven small entrances. The main tunnel is usually 10 to 12 feet (3 x 4m) long, with several branches, at least one nesting room and one or two food storage rooms.

A gerbil poses in front of its cage.

pens with hamsters, although gerbils do not reproduce quite so fast. It takes about 24 to 26 days for the babies to develop within the mother.

Gerbils live longer than their rodent relatives. The average life expectancy is 3 to 4 years, but some have been known to live as long as 7 or 8 years.

GERBIL BREEDING

The golden brownish-red agouti is the gerbil's original color, but cream, black, and white gerbils have also been bred. The first gerbil show of any size was held in London in 1971 by the National Mongolian Gerbil Society.

CHAPTER 6

FERRETS

The ferret is a member of the weasel family and is related to the mink, otter, sable, badger and skunk. It is larger than any of the rodent pets. Adult ferrets range from about 14 to 16 inches (35 to 40 cm) and weigh 1.5 to 5.0 pounds (0.8 to 2.5 kilograms).

The domestication of the ferret is a bit of a mystery. For one thing, the ferret that we know today as a pet does not exist in the wild. It was bred by people as a hunting animal so long ago that scientists cannot even be sure which animals were the ferret's ancestors. Scientific evidence points to two animals: the steppe polecat found in Siberia or the European polecat. The wild polecat is larger

**The ferret does not exist
in the wild.**

than the ferret, reaching a length of 21 in. (60 cm). All
three animals are so closely related that they can mate and
produce healthy offspring, just as dogs and wolves can.

The Egyptians are believed to have domesticated the
ferret, but no one is sure when. Estimates vary from 3000
B.C. to 300 B.C. Later, the Romans and the Chinese used
tamed ferrets to catch mice, rats, and other pests. Histori-
ans believe that European soldiers returning from the

Middle East brought the ferret to Europe between the years 900 and 1100.

BORN AND BRED TO HUNT

Europeans used ferrets to hunt rabbits and rodents. The ferrets were sent into the burrows to drive the animals out into the open. The people would wait outside with shovels and dogs and kill as many of the animals as they could.

When a hunt was over, the hunter or exterminator would call his ferret back by ringing a little bell or making some other sound to which the ferret had learned to respond. Sometimes a ferret would not respond and would stay down in the burrows, perhaps falling asleep in a cozy chamber. Then the hunter had no choice but to wait for the ferret to come out. Or, he could send another ferret inside to chase it. Some hunters tried tying a long line or leash to the ferret, but this didn't always work very well

This 700-year-old drawing shows a woman placing a ferret in a rabbit hole and the rabbit being flushed out on the other side.

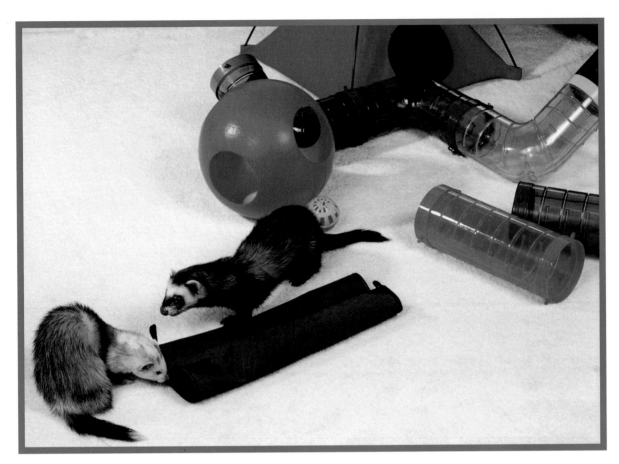

Ferrets love games and climbing through tubes.

because the line often became entangled on underground roots or rocks.

Ferrets became very popular in the United States in about 1875. A professional exterminator called a ferret man would rid buildings of mice and rats for a fee. He would bring a few ferrets in a box and release them into barns or basements to hunt. Sometimes he would close up all the holes in a house except one, so the rodents couldn't escape out the "back door" when the ferret came in. Ferrets have also been used in large cities to destroy rats that lived in sewer pipes.

BREEDING

Before the 1900s, all ferrets were bred as albinos. This made them easier to be seen and recaptured when taken out hunting. Today, pet ferrets come in many different colors. Sable, a brown color, is the most common. Other popular colors are gray, silver, cinnamon, siamese, chocolate, platinum, and even spotted.

Ferrets only became popular as pets in the last 20 years. Because they were bred as hunting animals, they still retain some wildness, even a little fierceness, in their personalities. The breeders of pet ferrets have succeeded to some extent in creating a gentler ferret. Some extremely tame ferrets will not even bother to chase a mouse. They can be affectionate and very playful pets. They are intelligent animals and love games that involve chasing, hiding, or tug-of-war. But they are known to nip their owners and, for this reason, they are not recommended as pets for young children.

CHAPTER 6

OR CAPTIVES PETS?

As we have seen, most small mammals are kept in cages. Some, like rabbits or ferrets, may spend a lot of time out of the cage and won't run away if they are sufficiently tame or attached to their owners. The smaller rodents, such as gerbils or mice, can be handled easily, but if they are let loose they cannot be expected to refrain from running away.

These animals exist in a kind of halfway state. They are not companions in the full sense of the word. They are captives, totally dependent on their owners for everything. Because of this, they are sometimes neglected. Once the novelty of the pet wears off—when the mouse or the

Almost all small rodents must be kept in cages.

guinea pig does not seem as fascinating as it first did—a young pet owner can begin to tire of the caring chores and become forgetful about changing the bedding in the cage and providing food and fresh water. An animal deprived of water will die. Often parents step in and take over these jobs, or the pet is given away or returned to the pet store.

But many owners of small mammals are quite devoted to them. For children, it is an opportunity to have a pet that is their very own. The animals are appreciated for their gentle natures, their adaptability, and their soft, furry coats.

51

In fact, because of this, some of the small mammals have been used in pet therapy. Pet therapy was developed when it was discovered that the pleasure people take in stroking and caring for pets has health benefits.

Now, in some hospitals and nursing homes, people who are lonely or sick or mentally ill can receive an animal to care for. It lifts their spirits and improves their health.

Are small mammals captives or pets? This question will probably never be answered. In some homes, small mammals are poisoned, hunted, or trapped. In other homes, they are an important, valued part of the family.

Quiet moments stroking a soft, cuddly pet can be very beneficial to a person's health.

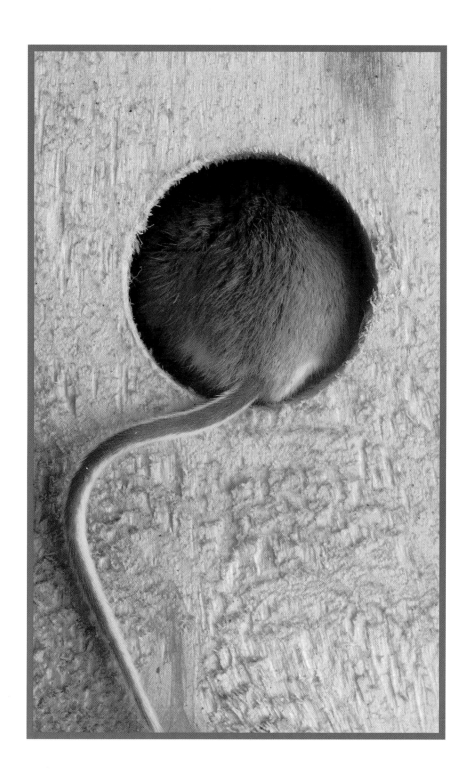

GLOSSARY

agouti The natural color of wild brown or reddish brown mice, rats, guinea pigs, and other small mammals.

albino A person or animal whose skin, hair, and eyes lack normal color. They have white skin, light-colored hair, and pink eyes.

archaeology The study of the way humans or animals lived a very long time ago.

archaeologists People who dig up the remains of ancient cities or settlements and study the bones, weapons, pottery, and other things they find. They also dig up the remains of animals and study their bones to understand how they lived and changed over time.

breed to reproduce by having offspring

bubonic plague A highly contagious disease that causes large lumps, or bubos, to appear in the armpit or groin of a person. It also causes fever, exhaustion, and delirium. Fleas from infected rats are the carriers.

carnivore Animal or plant that eats animals to survive.

cartilage A soft but strong tissue found between bones; your ears and nose are made of cartilage.

cavy A group of short-tailed rodents from South America that includes the guinea pig and the capybara.

conquistadors The Spanish conquerors of Mexico, Peru, and other parts of the Americas in the 1500s.

domestication The act of training or changing a wild animal so that it can be used by people.

mammals A group of animals that are warm-blooded, have some hair or fur, and nurse their young on milk.

rodent A group of mammals that have constantly growing incisors (teeth) that are used for gnawing.

selective breeding To pick specific animals to mate and have offspring in order to create an animal with a particular uniform appearance or behavior.

species A group of animals or plants, smaller than a genus, that have certain characteristics in common.

warm-blooded Animals that have body temperatures that stay approximately the same.

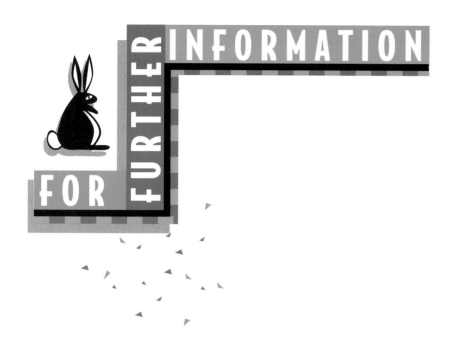

FOR FURTHER INFORMATION

BOOKS FOR ADVANCED READERS

Clutton-Brock, Juliet. *A Natural History of Domesticated Animals.* Austin: University of Texas Press, 1989.

Serpell, James. *In the Company of Animals: A History of Human Animal Relationships.* New York: B. Blackwell, 1986.

Villiard, Paul. *Raising Small Animals for Fun and Profit.* New York: Winchester Press, 1973

BOOKS FOR YOUNG READERS

Chrystie, Frances N. *Pets: A Complete Handbook.* Boston: Little, Brown and Co., 1964.

Dobrin, Arnold. *Gerbils.* New York: Lothrop, Lee & Shephard, 1970.

Fischer-Nagel, Heiderose and Andreas. *Inside the Burrow: The Life of the Golden Hamster.* Minneapolis: Carolrhoda Books, 1986.

Hess, Lilo. *Time for Ferrets.* New York: Charles Scribner's Sons, 1987.

King-Smith, Dick. *I Love Guinea Pigs.* Cambridge: Candlewick Press, 1994.

Morton, Chuck and Fox. *Ferrets: A Complete Pet Owner's Manual.* Hauppauge, NY: Barron's, 1985.

Robinson, D. G. *Gerbils.* Neptune City, NY: T. F. H. Publications, 1984.

Silverstein, Alvin and Virginia. *Guinea Pigs: All About Them.* New York: Lothrop, Lee & Shepard, 1972.

_____. *Hamsters: All About Them.* New York: Lothrop, Lee & Shepard, 1974.

Sproule, Anna and Michael. *Mice and Rats.* New York: The Bookwright Press, 1989.

Wexler, Jerome. *Pet Hamsters.* Morton Grove, IL: Albert Whitman & Co., 1992.

Wood, Gerald L. *Guinness Book of Pet Records.* Middlesex, Great Britain: Guinness Superlatives Ltd., 1984.

INTERNET SITES

Gerbil Information Page

http://users.bart.nl/~fredveen/gerbiluk.htm

This site provides extensive information about gerbils and their breeds.

American Fancy Rat and Mouse Association

http://www.pacificnet.net/afrma/

This organization's homepage provides links to other small mammal organizations and pages on rodent care.

Ferret Net

http://www.ferret.net/

This site has a list of ferret links to the web organized by topic.

House Rabbit Society

http://www.rabbit.org/

This organization educates the public on rabbit care and finds homes for orphaned or injured rabbits.

The Complete Hamster Site

http://www.ed.ac.uk/~eoas24/hamsters/hammain.htm

A site that has loads of photos and information on hamsters.

INDEX

Page numbers in *italics* indicate illustrations.

JOHN ZEAMAN is a journalist. For the past thirteen years, he has been a critic, feature writer, and editor with the *Bergen Record* of New Jersey. His interest in pets and animal domestication stems from the numerous pets that have lived in his household, including a standard poodle, two cats, gerbils, a parakeet, finches, lizards, turtles, a garter snake, and, briefly, a wild squirrel. The idea for this series grew out of a project that his daughter did in the fifth grade on the origins of pets. He lives in Leonia, New Jersey, with his wife, Janet, and their children, Claire and Alex.